TAMBA AND THE CHIEF

Man tram m'ump.
Let's tell a story.
Temne expression

For Megan
—M. L.

For Father Lemur
—C.R.

Tamba and the Chief is based on "The King, and His Daughter, and Mr. Tamba," from *A Collection of Temne Traditions, Fables and Proverbs,* by The Rev. C. F. Schlenker. London: The Church Missionary Society, 1861.

This tale is from the Temne culture of Sierra Leone.

© 1998 The Rourke Press, Inc.

ILLUSTRATIONS © Charles Reasoner

Library of Congress Cataloging-in-Publication Data

Lilly, Melinda.
   Tamba and the chief: [a Temne tale] / by Melinda Lilly;   illustrated by Charles Reasoner.
      p. cm. — (African tales and myths)
   Summary: While seeking the village of Chief Kotombo, Tamba offers aid to the animals he meets along the way, and later they return his kindness, enabling him to marry the chief's daughter.
   ISBN 1-57103-245-2
   [1. Temne (African people)—Folklore. 2. Folklore—Sierra Leone.] I. Reasoner, Charles, ill. II. Title III. Series: Lilly, Melinda. African tales and myths.
PZ8.1.L468Tam 1998
398.2'0899632—dc21   98–20326
                                                                                                          CIP
                                                                                                          AC

Printed in the USA

African Tales and Myths

TAMBA

AND THE CHIEF

A Temne Tale

Retold by
Melinda Lilly

Illustrated by
Charles Reasoner

The Rourke Press, Inc.
Vero Beach, Florida 32964

Tamba stood on the hillside bank of the swollen Rokel River, looking down at his flooded village. After his people had left, he had stayed to dig trenches and prevent further damage. But now his work was complete. "Spirit of the River," he said, "leave my village. Go back to your home so my people can return to theirs." He dropped grains of rice in the water, watching them float downriver as he walked to the marsh.

He stopped when he saw ants stranded on a drowned
millet stalk.

"Help us, Brother Tamba!" They scrambled up the
hand he offered to them.
"Thank you," they
chorused as he
returned them to
their tall anthill.

6

"Good-bye, my friends," said Tamba. "I'm going to Chief Kotombo's town to find help for the village."

"Chief Kotombo?" asked R'ak the ant. "Have you heard? He announced that any man may ask to marry his eldest daughter, Namina."

"I hadn't heard," said Tamba slowly. "But what could I offer a chief's daughter?"

"Yourself," said R'ak.

"Ha!" laughed Tamba. "Namina is said to be as beautiful as the sun and as wise as the elders. I have nothing fine enough to offer her and her family."

"If she is as wise as you say, she doesn't want fancy gifts," argued R'ak. "And a rich chief doesn't need them."

"Perhaps you're right, Sister R'ak," Tamba mused. "Peace and plenty to you."

7

Tamba walked out of the marsh and along the flooded paths of his village. Listening to the silence, he realized a chief's son-in-law could help life return to his people's home. With little to lose and much to gain, he decided to ask to marry the chief's daughter.

But what could he offer? He found peanuts and rice straw near the granary. Placing them in his basket, he could almost hear the songs sung at last year's harvest. He found a net and scooped up a fish, remembering the fisherwomen's graceful casting. He wondered if Namina would sense the spirit of his people in the humble gifts.

As he left the village, weaverbirds darted above him like flashes of sun. "Hello, Tra-Bamp," greeted Tamba. "How are you?"

"The storm tore our nests," they answered. "We're looking for dry grass so we can weave new homes."

"Would my straw help?" he offered. The flock swirled around him, then disappeared with the straw into the sky.

With a smile Tamba hiked on, coming to a tangled mangrove swamp.

When he stepped on a mossy log, the log said, "Please don't step on me. I'm not strong. Not enough food." The talking log was a crocodile!

"I'm sorry, Sister Kwi." Tamba stepped back. "But I have something you can eat."

"You?" she chortled. "You're too skinny for me to eat."

"Not me!" Tamba said quickly. "Have a fish!" Snap! Crunch! In one bite the fish was gone. Tamba hurried away carrying only his peanuts.

As he left the mangroves he saw the buildings of Chief Kotombo's town shining in the distance like turtles' backs. He continued on, following a path along the town's mud wall.

He walked through the gate and joined a crowd gathering in front of the chief's meetinghouse. To hungry Tamba, the round building of polished clay and thatch looked like a giant, golden cooking pot.

He searched the faces of the crowd. Everyone was as thin and worn as the people of his own village, but he recognized no one. "What's happening?" he asked a man standing nearby.

"Chief Kotombo will announce—" began the tall, gaunt man.

With a blast of horns the meetinghouse doors were thrown open. In a whirl of bright cloth and leopard skin, Chief Kotombo appeared and took his seat under the royal umbrella. His daughter Namina joined him, moving with a gazelle's grace. Tamba tried to see her face, but her hooded robe kept her in shadow.

Chief Kotombo spoke in a booming voice. "My daughter Namina has completed the Bundu rites of womanhood and is ready to marry, but she has refused all the men that have presented themselves to her. So now I will make the decision." Namina stiffened.

"The man who can guess what I keep in this amulet around my neck will marry my Namina," he said sternly. He waved his hand, dismissing his daughter. She disappeared inside the meetinghouse.

"Now, who will answer my challenge?" Chief Kotombo asked, scanning the crowd.

A warrior in a robe covered with amulets stepped forward with a swagger. "Mighty O-Bai, in your carved amulet is a finger bone of your enemy."

Chief Kotombo glared. "There is nothing left of my enemies! Away with you!"

A handsome man strutted at the front of the line. "The finest jewels—"

"I am not a bride bedecked with bangles!" snorted Chief Kotombo. "Out of my sight!"

14

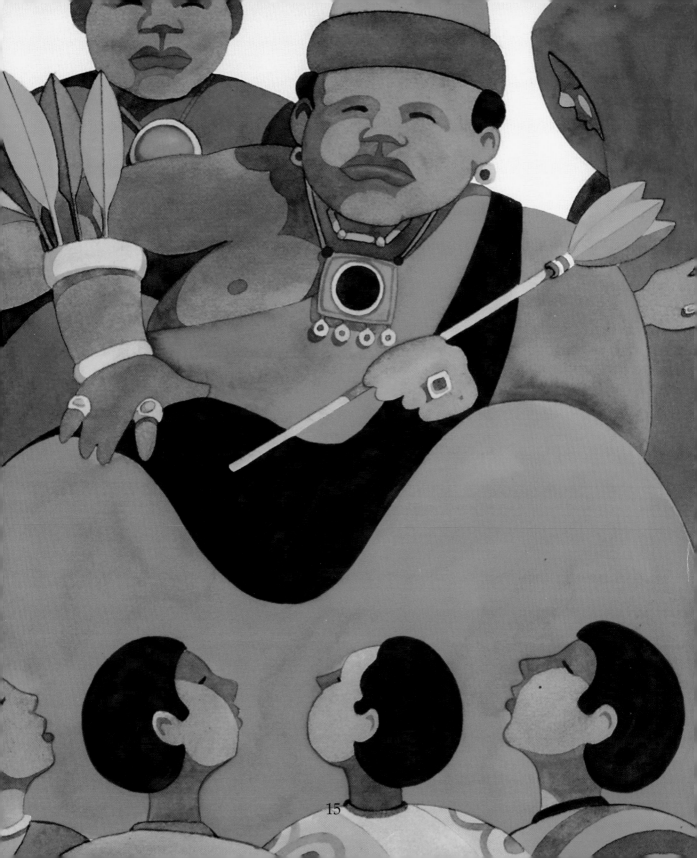

After considering the chief's challenge, Tamba slipped around the meetinghouse to ponder his answer. His quiet contemplation was interrupted by birds chattering near a door.

"She's forgotten to bring our food," complained Hornbill.

"What could be keeping her?" worried a flock of parrots.

"We're so hungry," chirped brightly colored turacos.

"Would you like my peanuts?" offered Tamba. The birds flew to him as a beautiful young woman opened the door.

She scattered nuts, saying, "I see you share my love for our feathered brothers and sisters."

Tamba nodded, drawn by the warmth in the woman's dark eyes. He lifted his hand, touching her fingertips in the Temne greeting. She held his hand and his gaze for a moment.

"Are you here for the royal guessing game?" she asked, pulling away.

"Yes," he admitted. "If I were the chief's son-in-law I could help my flooded village. But what do I know of a chief's amulet?"

"The answer lies in this riddle," she said. "What ties a chief to those of the past? What is the knot that always will last?" With a twinkle in her eye, she went inside before Tamba could respond.

"Sorry I can't help," Hornbill squawked, flying away. "Birds don't have those strings."

Tamba smiled. "But you have helped, my friend." With Hornbill's clue he had his answer!

When Chief Kotombo appeared the next morning, Tamba was waiting. He introduced himself and recited:

> What ties a chief to those of the past?
> What is the knot that always will last?
> In the pouch of the great Temne king
> Is the royal cord—your navel string!

"You answer true!" grinned the chief, eyeing Tamba's worn robe. "But a beggar does not marry a king's daughter so easily. I have another test for you."

Chief Kotombo clapped his hands. A servant approached, bowing. "Bring the fiber," the chief ordered. A long line of servants filed past carrying mounds of cord. "The royal fishnets are torn," said Chief Kotombo. "Tamba, to marry Namina you must knot ten nets by morning." Disappointed, Tamba bowed and turned away, slowly walking toward the mountain of fiber.

"Tamba!" the weaverbirds cried as they landed in front of him on the pile. "Are you weaving a nest like ours?"

"No, friends, I need to make ten fishnets by morning," he said.

"Let us help you as you helped us," they offered. The birds fluttered, covering the cords as they nipped and tied the nets.

The next morning Tamba proudly presented the king with ten beautiful nets. "Well done," remarked Chief Kotombo, fingering them in disbelief, "but I have another task for you. In the night, a turtle stole a bell from my stool. Find it by sundown if you wish to marry Namina."

amba bowed to the chief and left to search the mangroves without much hope for success. "Sister Kwi?" he called, slogging through the swamp. "Help me, my friend! A turtle has stolen the king's bell and I must find it."

The crocodile surfaced with a toothy grin. "I know the turtle! His nest is tucked in the knee roots of the thicket. Wait here while I . . . persuade him to give me the bell."

The next day, Tamba returned to the meetinghouse joyfully ringing the king's bell. "So you've brought it," said Chief Kotombo, silencing the bell. "I have one more task for you, follow me." He walked around the building and pulled open a door, unleashing an avalanche of grain. "You are to separate my rice from my millet by morning. Then you may ask to marry my daughter."

He clapped his hands and two muscular warriors appeared. "Ya Fura and Ya Koro will stand outside while you work. No visitors." Chief Kotombo shut the door and Tamba was left alone.

25

Discouraged, he sank into the ocean of grain. He noticed ants crawling along the wall, then sat up suddenly. "Tr'ak, my ant friends, the chief wants the grain separated. Can you help me put the rice in one pile and the millet in another?"

"Of course, Brother Tamba," they answered.

Through the night, the ants and Tamba sorted the grain one kernel at a time. The piles grew until they touched the ceiling.

As sunlight peeked in the storeroom, the door was thrown open. Chief Kotombo and his daughter Namina admired the towering heaps of millet and rice. Behind them, curious townspeople gaped at the abundance of grain.

"There's a storeroom of food!" the crowd exclaimed in surprise. "Tamba, thank you for sharing with the hungry!"

"It is your generous chief who shares with you," Tamba said hopefully. "Not I."

"Thank you, wise Kotombo!" the people yelled. "Kori-u, wise Kotombo!"

Chief Kotombo's face softened as he looked at his cheering subjects and beautiful daughter. "There's food for all," he announced. "Today we celebrate the wedding of Tamba and Namina."

Tamba smiled at Namina with happiness and surprise. Once again, he felt the warmth in her dark eyes and touched his fingertips to hers in the Temne greeting.

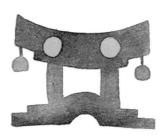

31

PRONUNCIATION AND DEFINITION GUIDE:

Bundu (BOON doo): A West African secret society for women.

Fura (FEWR uh): A fictional Temne warrior.

Kori-u (KOR i-OO): Temne for "I salute you!"

Koro (KOR oh): A fictional Temne warrior.

Kotombo (Koh TOHM Boh): A fictional Temne chief.

kwi (KWIH): The Temne word for crocodile.

Namina (NAHM´ i NAH): A fictional Temne woman.

O-Bai (O-bie): The title of the Temne head chief.

r'ak (r AHK): The Temne word for ant. The plural form of r'ak is tr'ak.

Rokel (RO kel) River: A river in Sierra Leone.

Tamba (TAHM bah): A Temne fictional hero.

Temne (TEM nee): A culture and language of Sierra Leone.

tra bamp (trah BAMP): African weaverbirds.

turaco also **touraco** (TOOR´ uh COE): An African cuckoo.

Ya (YAH): The Temne equivalent of mister.